Momma, Don't Worry

Written & Illustrated by
Malana Bracht

MOMMA, DON'T WORRY

Copyright © 2022 by MALANA BRACHT

All rights reserved. No part of this book may be used or reproduced in any manner whatsoever without written permission, except in the case of brief quotations embodied in critical articles or reviews.

Thank you for buying an authorized edition of this book and for complying with copyright laws by not reproducing, scanning, or distributing any part of it in any form without permission. You are supporting writers and their hard work by doing this. The resources in this book are provided for encouragement and informational purposes only and should not be used to replace the specialized training of a healthcare or mental health professional. Neither the author nor the publisher can be held responsible for the use of this information within this book. Please, if you are struggling with mental or physical health concerns, always consult a trained professional before making any decisions regarding the treatment of yourself or others.

For more information, contact:
Malana Bracht at www.malanabracht.com
Written and Illustrated by Malana Bracht

ISBN: 9798838030092 (paperback)
Printed in The United States of America
First Edition: August 2022

To Jesus, who healed me and redeemed
my perspective of motherhood.

To every new and expectant momma-
the Lord sees you and so do I.

To the many mothers in my life who
birthed different parts of me, thank you.

To my loving husband, Travis- thank you
for always believing in me.

To Gracia, Holten, Lincoln, and Stephen-
the Littles who made me "Momma"-
I will always love you.

Conception to 6 Weeks Gestation

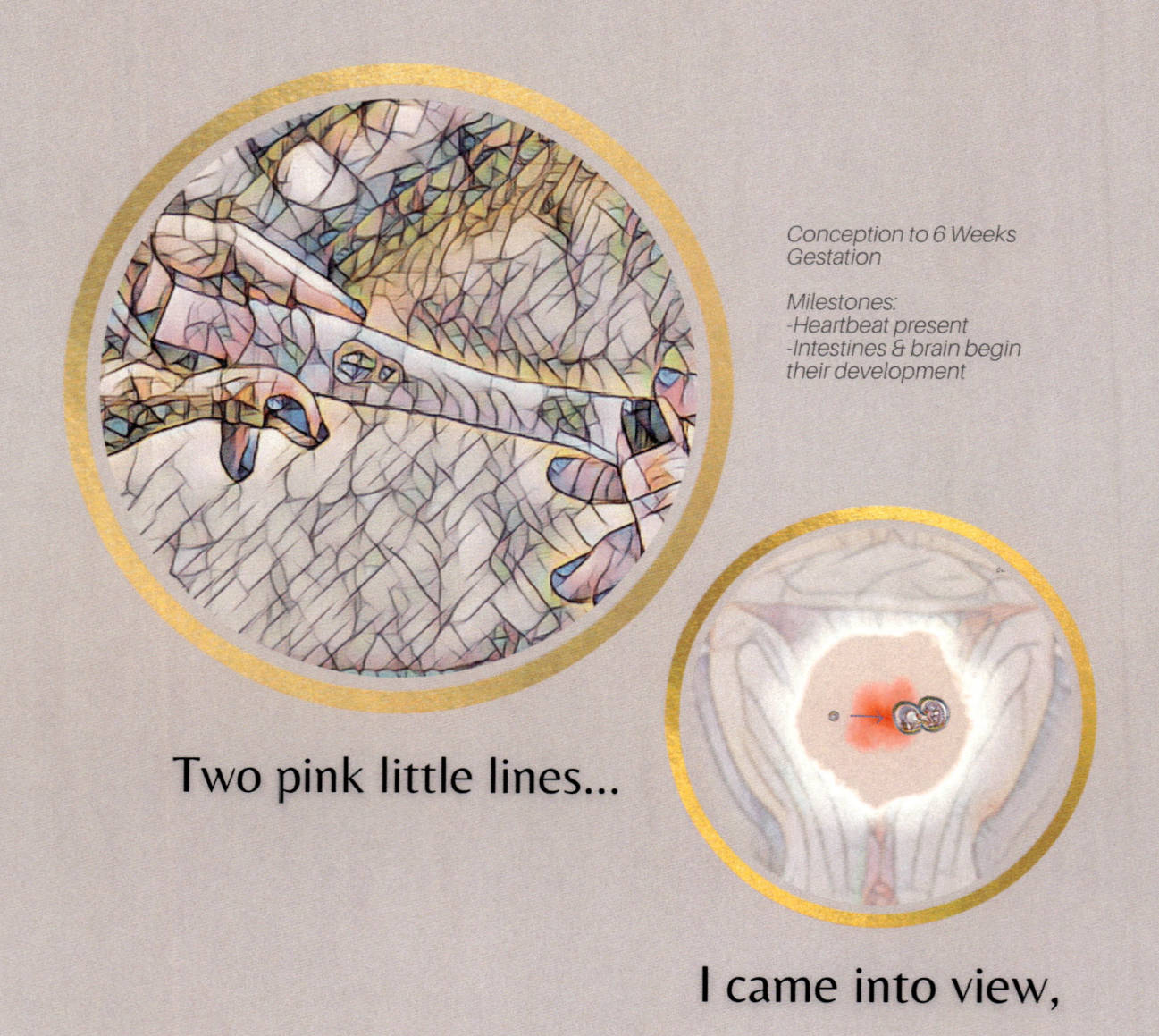

Milestones:
-Heartbeat present
-Intestines & brain begin their development

Two pink little lines...

I came into view,

...our Heavenly Father began knitting me in your womb.

Joy, excitement...
nervousness and fear,
nausea, super smell,
tiredness and tears...

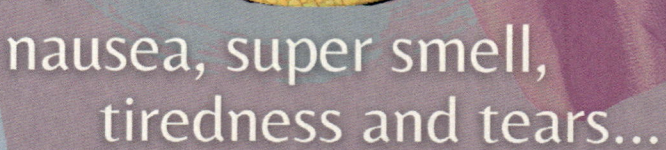

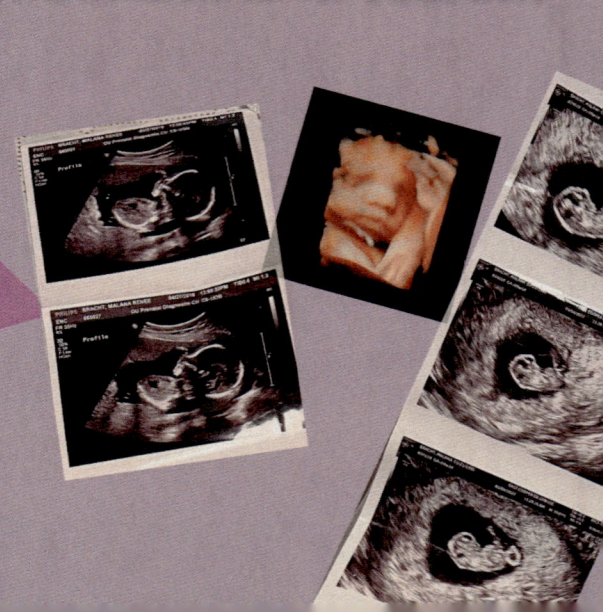

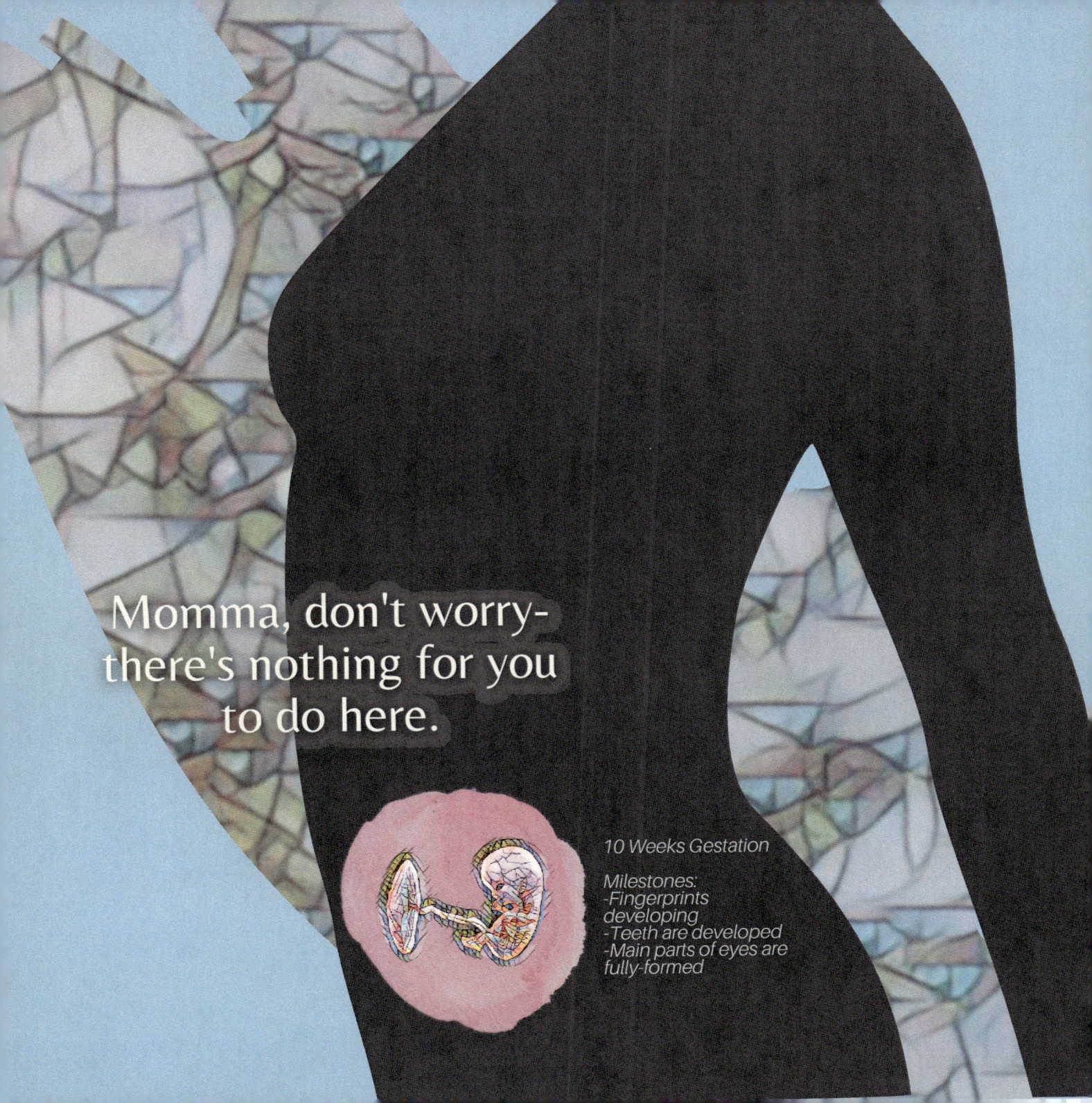

Momma, don't worry— there's nothing for you to do here.

10 Weeks Gestation

Milestones:
- Fingerprints developing
- Teeth are developed
- Main parts of eyes are fully-formed

-buy diapers & wipes....
-hang mobile...
-install carseat...
-wash baby's clothes...
-buy baby book...

You make lists and plans, and prepare a place to be...

But Momma, don't worry- Papa God is taking care of me!

14 Weeks Gestation

Milestones:
- Baby's reproductive organs are recognizable on ultrasound
- Baby has fingerprints
- If it is a girl, her ovaries already have over 2 million eggs
- Kidneys are working
- Hair follicles are forming
- Kicks may be strong enough to feel

Searching for my perfect name...

...not knowing if I'm a John or a Jane,

Tulip?

No.

Juliet?

No.

You've got to pick something!

22 Weeks Gestation

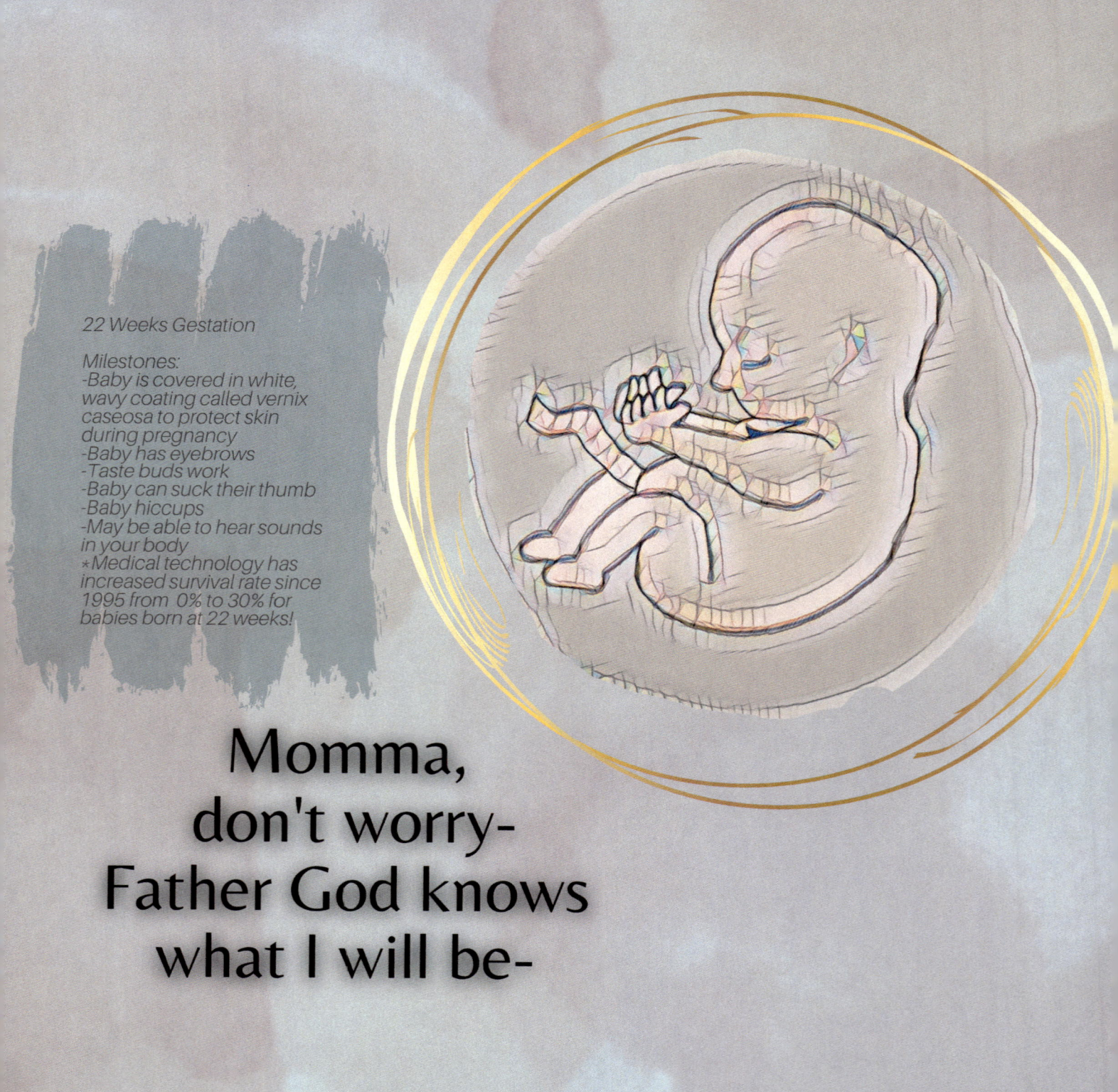

Milestones:
-Baby is covered in white, wavy coating called vernix caseosa to protect skin during pregnancy
-Baby has eyebrows
-Taste buds work
-Baby can suck their thumb
-Baby hiccups
-May be able to hear sounds in your body
*Medical technology has increased survival rate since 1995 from 0% to 30% for babies born at 22 weeks!

Momma, don't worry- Father God knows what I will be-

"It's a..."

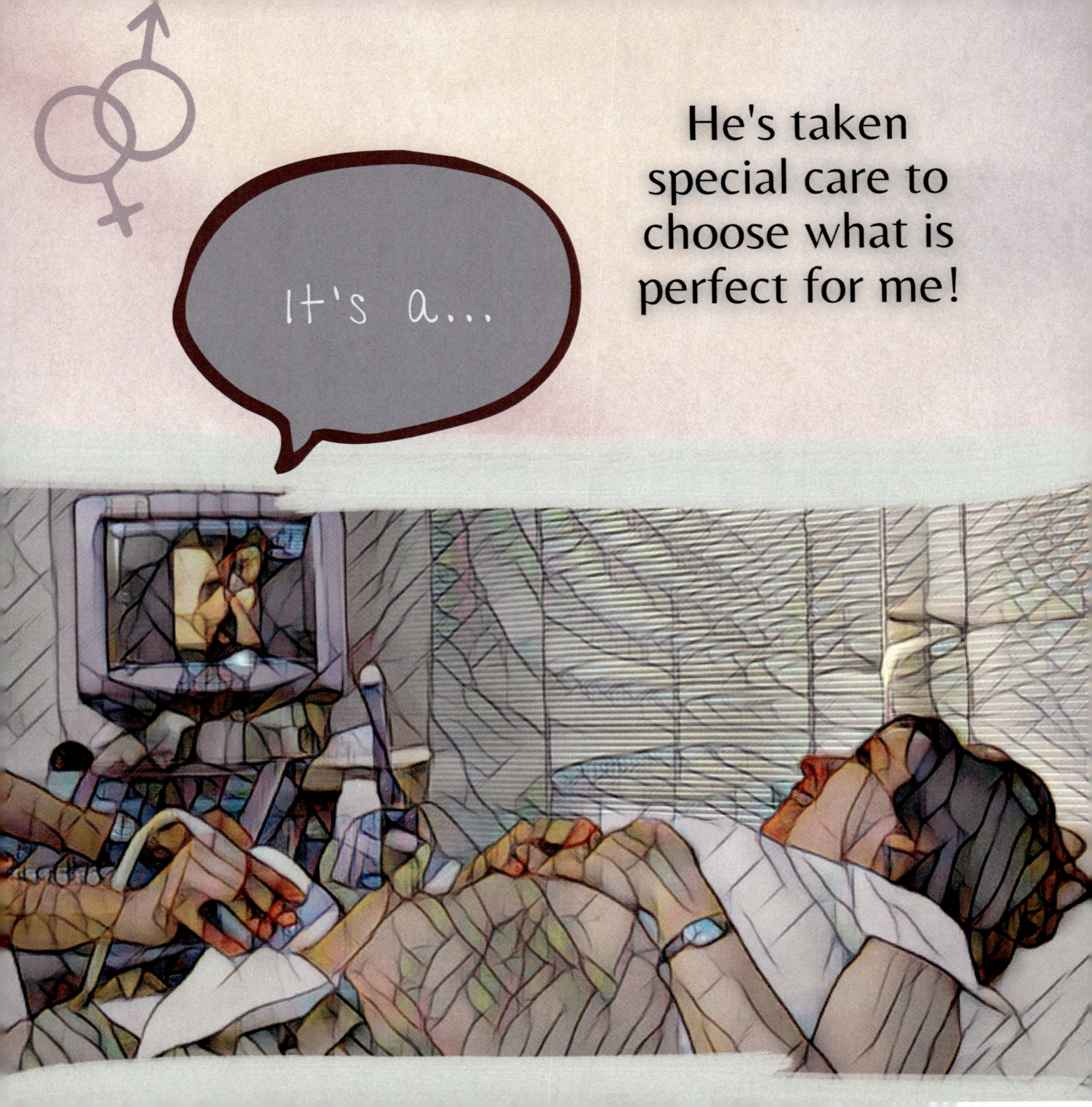

He's taken special care to choose what is perfect for me!

I hear you when you laugh,

I hear you when you cry...

Even though I can't talk yet,
I'll remind you, "I love you"
from inside.

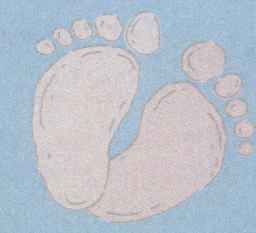

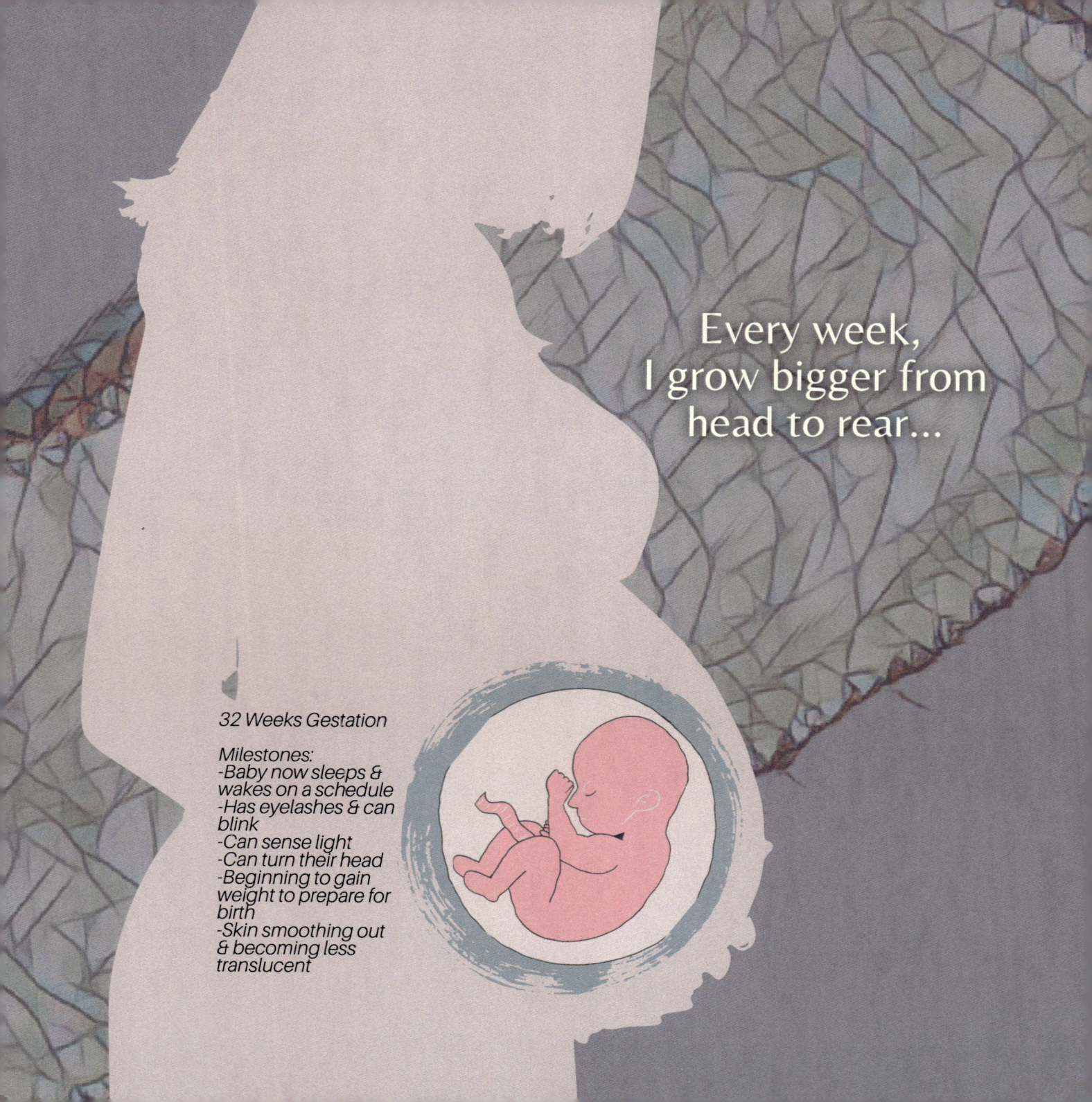

Every week,
I grow bigger from
head to rear...

32 Weeks Gestation

Milestones:
-Baby now sleeps & wakes on a schedule
-Has eyelashes & can blink
-Can sense light
-Can turn their head
-Beginning to gain weight to prepare for birth
-Skin smoothing out & becoming less translucent

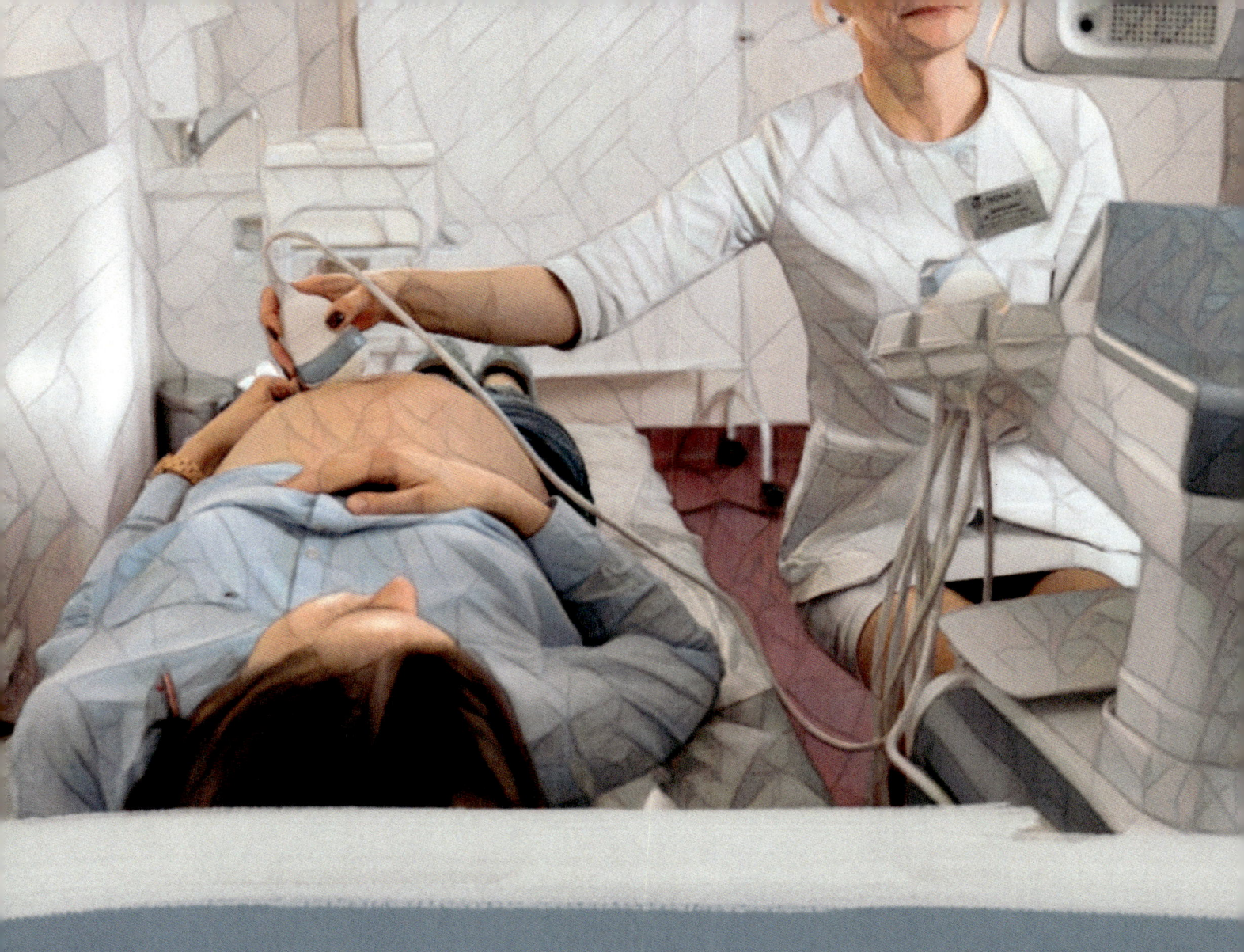

Every week, my due date draws even more near...

Every week you wonder when I'll be here...

37 Weeks Gestation

Milestones:
- Lungs are fully formed
- Inhaling & exhaling amniotic fluid to prepare for breathing & swallowing after birth
- Can grasp small objects like toes

*Considered full-term

But Momma, don't worry- Daddy God will help you persevere!

The Lord up above is finishing my inward parts...

and knows the perfect timing for when labor will start.

39 Weeks Gestation

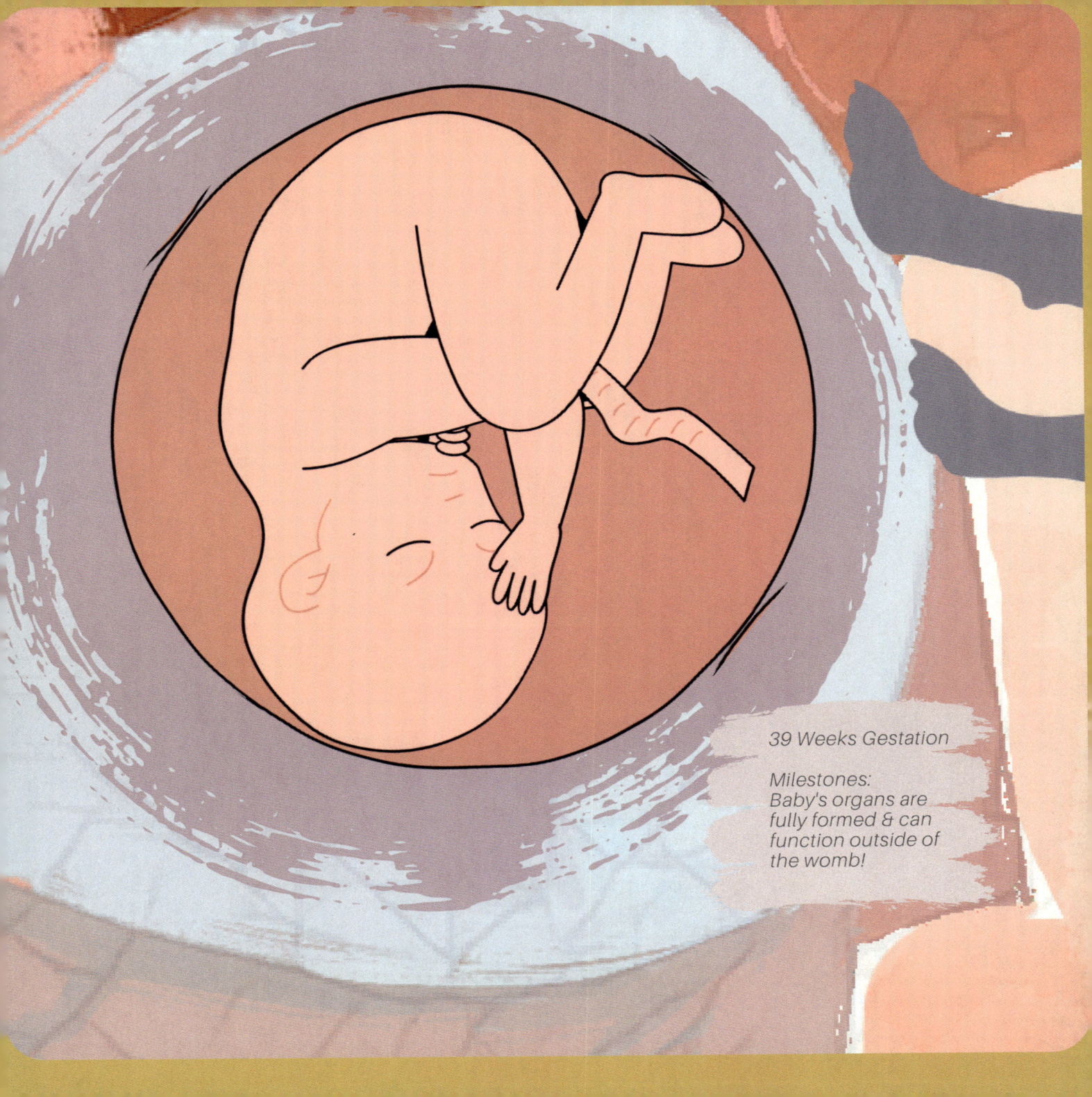

Milestones: Baby's organs are fully formed & can function outside of the womb!

So whether it is thirty-nine weeks and five days...

or forty-one and two,

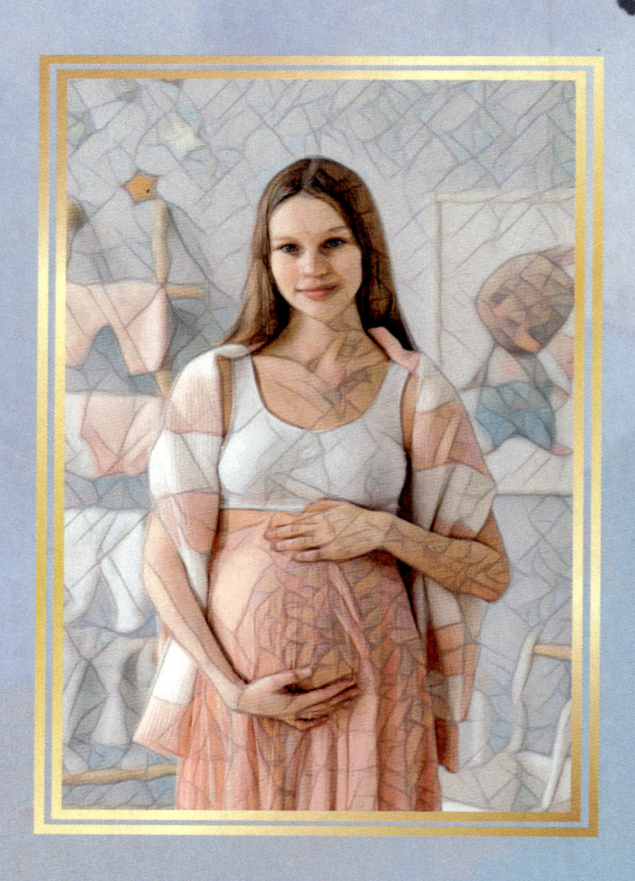

*Fun Fact:
Not all babies are born on their due date! Many mommas could go into labor from 38-42 weeks of pregnancy!*

Vaginal Birth

Home Birth

...it will be the perfect timing (and path) to make my way to you!

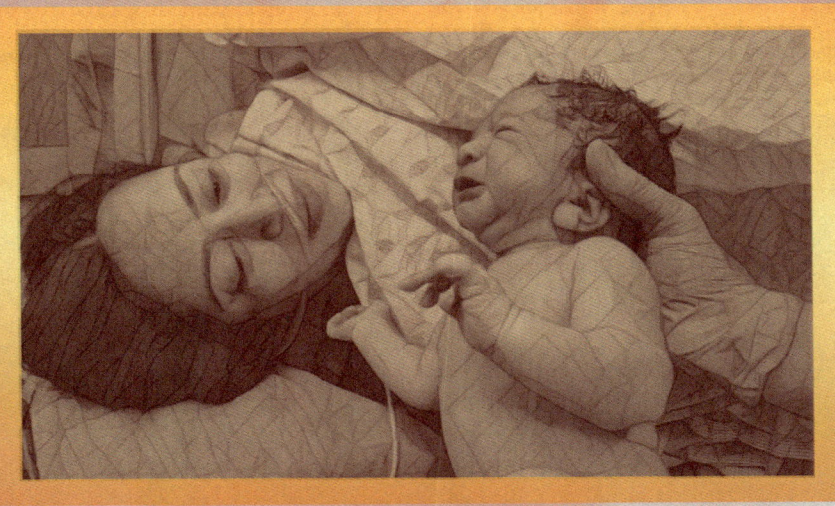

Cesarean Section

Don't worry about the years ahead,

the tears, the smiles,

what you wish you knew...

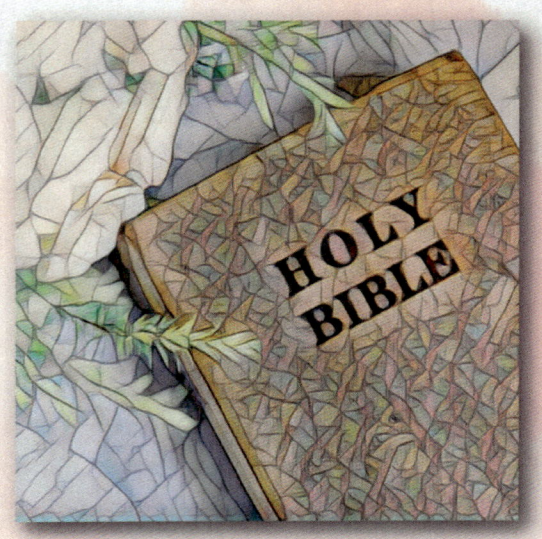

Cast your cares on the One who made me throughout your motherhood...

...and He will show you what to do!

My Motherhood Journey

Baby's Name: _____ Due Date: _____

When I found out I was pregnant, I felt _____

At the time, I lived in _____ , worked at _____ ,

and attended church at _____ .

My symptoms during early pregnancy were _____

My biggest food craving(s): _____

Baby names I liked _____

I plan to find out the gender of baby ☐ yes ☐ no   Baby is a... _____

When I first heard baby's heartbeat & saw baby on ultrasound, I felt _____
_____
_____

My hopes as baby grows _____
_____
_____

Baby arrived on: _____ Weight: _____ Length: _____

Time of Birth: _____ Location: _____

Prayer of Blessing Over You & Your Baby

(Pray it out loud like you believe it ♡)

Heavenly Father,

I thank you for this new life inside of me and for choosing me as their momma!
I know I cannot do this alone and ask for your help as I raise this baby to honor you.
I thank you for every day I get to love this little life.
I ask and receive in faith your wisdom and guidance for raising this child.

By standing in faith and trusting on the promises of your Word, I declare that my pregnancy will go smoothly with minimal symptoms and childbirth will be swift, peaceful, with little pain and no complications!

I ask that your angels watch over the doctors and midwives as they help bring baby into this world and give me and baby the strength to endure.

In the name of Jesus, I command all fear and anxiety from the enemy to leave me in Jesus name and I invite your peace. Bring your peaceful presence in my heart and mind!
This new life as momma will not be easy, but I know you will be with me.
I will not always have the answers, but I know you and your Word will guide me.
Thank you that any need I have- you will take care of it all!

I recognize this baby is not my own, but yours that I have been given the privilege to raise.
Guide me, lead me, help me to know the depths of the love you have for me so I can love my baby as you have loved me.

I believe I can enjoy peace in my season of pregnancy and my years of growing into a mother.
If you are for me, nothing can be against me and my baby!

My family will be the first and not the last, we will be blessed when we get up and blessed when we lie down. We will be blessed when we leave and blessed when we come home. The work of my hands in motherhood and the workplace are blessed. My thoughts are blessed. The steps of my feet are blessed! My emotions do not lead me, but your Spirit does!
My body, finances, family, and future are BLESSED!

Thank you for my future that is full of hope- because you will be there.
In Jesus name,
Amen

Bible Promises for Pregnancy & Motherhood

→

Bible Promises for Pregnancy & Motherhood

"Consequently, faith comes from hearing the message, and the message is heard through the word about Christ." -Romans 10:17 NIV

Worry About Not Having Enough

- "The Lord is my shepherd, I lack nothing." -Psalms 23:1 NIV
- "Therefore I tell you, do not worry about your life, what you will eat or drink; or about your body, what you will wear. Is not life more than food, and the body more than clothes? Look at the birds of the air; they do not sow or reap or store away in barns, and yet your heavenly Father feeds them. Are you not much more valuable than they? Can any one of you by worrying add a single hour to your life?" -Matthew 6:25-17 NIV
- "I was young and now I am old, yet I have never seen the righteous forsaken or their children begging bread." -Psalm 37:25 NIV
- "And my God will meet all your needs according to the riches of his glory in Christ Jesus." -Philippians 4:19 NIV
- "Give, and it will be given to you. A good measure, pressed down, shaken together and running over, will be poured into your lap. For with the measure you use, it will be measured to you." -Luke 6:38 NIV
- "If you fully obey the Lord your God and carefully follow all his commands I give you today, The Lord will grant you abundant prosperity—in the fruit of your womb, the young of your livestock and the crops of your ground—in the land he swore to your ancestors to give you...The Lord will open the heavens, the storehouse of his bounty, to send rain on your land in season and to bless all the work of your hands. You will lend to many nations but will borrow from none."   -Deuteronomy 28:1,11-12 NIV

Overcoming Fear and Anxiety

- "There is no fear in love. But perfect love drives out fear, because fear has to do with punishment. The one who fears is not made perfect in love." -1 John 4:18 NIV
- "Do not be anxious about anything, but in every situation, by prayer and petition, with thanksgiving, present your requests to God. And the peace of God, which transcends all understanding, will guard your hearts and your minds in Christ Jesus." -Philippians 4:6-7 NIV
- "Whoever dwells in the shelter of the Most High will rest in the shadow of the Almighty. I will say of the LORD, "He is my refuge and my fortress, my God, in whom I trust." Surely he will save you from the fowler's snare and from the deadly pestilence...You will not fear the terror of night, nor the arrow that flies by day, nor the pestilence that stalks in the darkness, nor the plague that destroys at midday." -Psalm 91:1-3, 5-6 NIV
- "Be strong and courageous. Do not be afraid or terrified because of them, for the LORD your God goes with you; he will never leave you nor forsake you." -Deuteronomy 31:6 NIV
- "Cast all your anxiety on him because he cares for you." 1 Peter 5:7 NIV

Continued...

You and Your Child's Worth in God's Eyes

- "For this is what the LORD Almighty says: "After the Glorious One has sent me against the nations that have plundered you-- for whoever touches you touches the apple of his eye-" -Zechariah 2:8 NIV
- "For we are God's handiwork, created in Christ Jesus to do good works, which God prepared in advance for us to do." -Ephesians 2:10 NIV
- Children are a heritage from the Lord, offspring a reward from him. Like arrows in the hands of a warrior are children born in one's youth. Blessed is the man whose quiver is full of them..." Psalm 127:3-5 NIV
- For you created my inmost being; you knit me together in my mother's womb.I praise you because I am fearfully and wonderfully made; your works are wonderful, I know that full well." -Psalm 139:13-14 NIV
- "Before I formed you in the womb I knew you, before you were born I set you apart; I appointed you as a prophet to the nations." -Jeremiah 1:5 NIV
- "How precious to me are your thoughts, God! How vast is the sum of them! Were I to count them, they would outnumber the grains of sand—when I awake, I am still with you." -Psalm 139-17-18 NIV
- "Indeed, the very hairs of your head are all numbered. Don't be afraid; you are worth more than many sparrows." -Luke 12:7 NIV

Biblical Promises for Your Health and Safety of You and Your Baby

- "If you say, "The LORD is my refuge," and you make the Most High your dwelling, no harm will overtake you, no disaster will come near your tent. For he will command his angels concerning you to guard you in all your ways; they will lift you up in their hands, so that you will not strike your foot against a stone. 'Because he loves me," says the LORD, "I will rescue him; I will protect him, for he acknowledges my name. He will call on me, and I will answer him; I will be with him in trouble, I will deliver him and honor him." Psalms 91:9-12, 14-15 NIV
- "Dear friend, I pray that you may enjoy good health and that all may go well with you, even as your soul is getting along well." 3 John 1:2
- "If you fully obey the Lord your God and carefully follow all his commands I give you today, the Lord your God will set you high above all the nations on earth. 2 All these blessings will come on you and accompany you if you obey the Lord your God: You will be blessed in the city and blessed in the country. The fruit of your womb will be blessed..." -Deuteronomy 28:1-4 NIV
- "His divine power has given us everything we need for a godly life through our knowledge of him who called us by his own glory and goodness. Through these he has given us his very great and precious promises, so that through them you may participate in the divine nature, having escaped the corruption in the world caused by evil desires." -2 Peter 1:3-4 NIV

Pregnancy Symptom Relief and Healing from Sickness/Disease

- "He makes me lie down in green pastures, he leads me beside quiet waters, he refreshes my soul." -Psalms 23:2 NIV
- ."I can do all things through Christ who strengthens me." -Philippians 4:13 NIV
- "In peace I will lie down and sleep for you alone, Lord, make me dwell in safety." -Psalm 4:8 NIV
- "But he was pierced for our transgressions, he was crushed for our iniquities; the punishment that brought us peace was upon him, and by his wounds we are healed. We all, like sheep, have gone astray, each of us has turned to his own way; and the LORD has laid on him the iniquity of us all." -Isaiah 53:5-6 NIV
- "Great crowds came to him, bringing the lame, the blind, the crippled, the mute and many others, and laid them at his feet; and he healed them." -Matthew 15:30 NIV
- "And these signs shall follow them that believe; In my name shall they cast out devils; they shall speak with new tongues; They shall take up serpents; and if they drink any deadly thing, it shall not hurt them; they shall lay hands on the sick, and they shall recover." -Mark 16:17-18 NIV
- "Truly I tell you, if anyone says to this mountain, 'Go, throw yourself into the sea,' and does not doubt in their heart but believes that what they say will happen, it will be done for them." -Mark 11:23 NIV
- "If you listen carefully to the LORD your God and do what is right in his eyes, if you pay attention to his commands and keep all his decrees, I will not bring on you any of the diseases I brought on the Egyptians, for I am the LORD, who heals you." -Exodus 15:26 NIV
- "Submit yourselves therefore to God. Resist the devil, and he will flee from you." -James 4:7 NIV
- "Now to him who is able to do immeasurably more than all we ask or imagine, according to his power that is at work within us, to him be glory in the church and in Christ Jesus throughout all generations, for ever and ever!" -Ephesians 3:20 NIV

For Wisdom in Decisions

- "In their hearts humans plan their course, but the LORD establishes their steps." -Proverbs 16:9 NIV
- "If any of you lacks wisdom, you should ask God, who gives generously to all without finding fault, and it will be given to you." -James 1:5 NIV
- "The fear of the Lord is the beginning of wisdom, and knowledge of the Holy One is understanding." -Proverbs 9:10 NIV
- "Therefore everyone who hears these words of mine and puts them into practice is like a wise man who built his house on the rock." -Matthew 7:24 NIV
- "Walk with the wise and become wise, for a companion of fools suffers harm." -Proverbs 13:20 NIV
- "Where there is strife, there is pride, but wisdom is found in those who take advice." -Proverbs 13:10 NIV
- "To the person who pleases him, God gives wisdom, knowledge and happiness, but to the sinner he gives the task of gathering and storing up wealth to hand it over to the one who pleases God." -Ecclesiastes 2:26 NIV

Fear that God is Mad at You

- "Beloved, let us love one another, for love is from God, and whoever loves has been born of God and knows God. Anyone who does not love does not know God, because God is love. In this the love of God was made manifest among us, that God sent his only Son into the world, so that we might live through him." -1 John 4:7-9 NIV
- If we confess our sins, he is faithful and just and will forgive us our sins and purify us from all unrighteousness." -1 John 1:9 NIV
- "The Lord is gracious and compassionate, slow to anger and rich in love."-Psalm 145:8 NIV
- "Let us then approach God's throne of grace with confidence, so that we may receive mercy and find grace to help us in our time of need." -Hebrews 4:16 NIV
- "What, then, shall we say in response to these things? If God is for us, who can be against us?" -Romans 8:31 NIV
- "The Lord appeared to us in the past, saying: "I have loved you with an everlasting love; I have drawn you with unfailing kindness." -Jeremiah 31:3 NIV
- "This righteousness is given through faith in Jesus Christ to all who believe. There is no difference between Jew and Gentile, for all have sinned and fall short of the glory of God," -Romans 3:22-23 NIV
- "We implore you on behalf of Christ: Be reconciled to God. God made him who had no sin to be sin for us, so that in him we might become the righteousness of God." -2 Corinthians 5:21 NIV
- "For God so loved the world that he gave his one and only Son, that whoever believes in him shall not perish but have eternal life. For God did not send his Son into the world to condemn the world, but to save the world through him. Whoever believes in him is not condemned, but whoever does not believe stands condemned already because they have not believed in the name of God's one and only Son." -John 3:16-18 NIV
- "In [Jesus] and through faith in him we may approach God with freedom and confidence." -Ephesians 3:12 NIV
- "He is patient with you, not wanting anyone to perish, but everyone to come to repentance." -2 Peter 2:3 NIV

Biblical Promises For Your Future When You Follow Him

- "And we know that in all things God works for the good of those who love him, who have been called according to his purpose." -Romans 8:28 NIV
- "For I know the plans I have for you," declares the Lord, "plans to prosper you and not to harm you, plans to give you hope and a future." -Jeremiah 29:11 NIV
- "Trust in the LORD with all your heart and do not lean on your own understanding. In all your ways acknowledge Him, and He will make your paths straight." Proverbs 3:5-6 NIV
- "The Lord will make you the head, not the tail. If you pay attention to the commands of the Lord your God that I give you this day and carefully follow them, you will always be at the top, never at the bottom. Do not turn aside from any of the commands I give you today, to the right or to the left, following other gods and serving them." -Deuteronomy 28:13-14 NIV
- "She is clothed with strength and dignity; she can laugh at the days to come." -Proverbs 31:25 NIV

Meet the Author

Photo Credit: Wendy Carey Photography | Charleston, SC

Author, Malana Bracht is "Momma" to four captivating children. Though she gained her Bachelor's Degree in Family Life Education, she never imagined writing and illustrating stories about motherhood! Birthing three children in three years and expecting her fourth in August 2022, she is no stranger to the journey to motherhood and the beautiful nuances and anxieties that come when expecting a child. She intimately understands that motherhood is not a perfect journey, but a practice that requires reliance on the Lord and his promises for parents in His word. Malana prays that she can encourage new and expectant moms as they prepare for their journey to birth their children as they themselves are birthed as mothers!

You can typically find Malana drinking iced coffee and pursuing some new project as she balances motherhood, being a minister's wife, writing, and entrepreneurship. You can connect more with her on social media or her website, www.malanabracht.com

Made in the USA
Columbia, SC
07 September 2022